Invest in Yourself

A Real-Life Story
with lessons for you
and your family.

by

Richard Houston

CONTENTS

COPYRIGHT

DISCLAIMER

DEDICATION

Even though I wrote this book, I certainly did not do it on my own. In fact, the information in this book comes from a range of people whom I love very dearly and who allowed me to do this.

To my loving children Beck, Destiny and Stefan, I thank you and love you all so very much. Thanks for all your interruptions and attempts to capture my attention.

To my darling Dragana, I thank you and love you for so much, but in this case for the numerous coffees and chats we have to analyse the world's problems and provide solutions. Your great insights and instincts really do help me to complete my understanding of this world.

(To the reader: if you ever get a chance to have a chat with my partner Dragana, you will understand everything I have said and know how understated I have been in my praise of her here.)

Thanks to all my loving family.

COPYRIGHT

DISCLAIMER

DEDICATION

Even though I wrote this book, I certainly did not do it on my own. In fact, the information in this book comes from a range of people whom I love very dearly and who allowed me to do this.

To my loving children Beck, Destiny and Stefan, I thank you and love you all so very much. Thanks for all your interruptions and attempts to capture my attention.

To my darling Dragana, I thank you and love you for so much, but in this case for the numerous coffees and chats we have to analyse the world's problems and provide solutions. Your great insights and instincts really do help me to complete my understanding of this world.

(To the reader: if you ever get a chance to have a chat with my partner Dragana, you will understand everything I have said and know how understated I have been in my praise of her here.)

Thanks to all my loving family.

ABOUT RICHARD HOUSTON

My name is Richard Houston. I am just an average guy who has taken the time to listen, look and learn. I have made more mistakes than anyone I know in life, and yet still, amazingly, I am here today to share with you my opinions and insights.

So what are my qualifications? Basically, I completed my High School Certificate in 1979 and attempted to obtain a Commerce Degree at the prestigious Melbourne University in 1980.

I learned early in my first economics class that I was not into this stuff and that there must be something more enjoyable to do with my time.

So I quit university and started my own business. I saw an advertisement in the "business for sale" column of the daily paper for a vending machine business. I went to see a man who said he had six vending machines located in local football clubs, and that they were making good money.

It sounded pretty good to a young man who wanted to make money, so I said I was in. He arranged a loan for $25,000, and thus I started my first business. To this day I still don't know how a young unemployed university student could get a loan for $25,000 from a major bank.

Well, the money came flowing in and within 12 months I had paid back the loan...and then *smack,* my first lesson in business. The government changed its rules and outlawed poker machines, and the business became worthless overnight.

Not to be deterred, I went off and got a job. I know, how pathetic of me, but hey, I was *just above broke* (JOB) and needed the money. So I did the right thing. I worked hard and saved money. I raised enough cash to buy my new business, a cigarette vending machine run.

I was confident that this time the government could not stop me. So off I went and bought the first five machines. In less than a year, I had some 20 machines stationed in local sporting clubs around my city.

Then it happened. The government stepped in again. It did not close me down, but they raised the prices to a point where the price of a pack of cigarettes was over $2.00 and my old machines could not handle so many coins. I had the choice of closing down again or spend thousands for the new machines that could handle the coins and notes.

The lesson I learned here was that technology can close you down as quickly as the government can.

By now, my decision to quit university was not looking so good. But still not to be deterred, off I went and began a career in finance. I started work for AVCO Finance (later bought out by GE Finance) and worked hard for two years until I became an assistant manager.

Along with the income from AVCO, my work at a second job at the cinema, and the money I received from playing football, I saved enough money to buy my first property and started living in it.

Now came my big move into banking. In 1987, just before the stock market crash, I started work with a major trading bank in Australia. I was fairly successful in my banking career, but I knew there was more.

Finally, in 1995, I left the bank with money in hand from my hard-earned savings and invested in a building technology, which my partner and I took to Asia.

Let's just say that the next four years was a nightmare. I went from owning a modest home and having a good income to nearly bankrupt.

We had spent all our money on getting a contract signed and sealed for 10,000 homes to be built in the Maldives, using our building technology, only to have the contract annulled by a certain Malaysian politician (who I think actually stole the deal).

Don't get me wrong—I am not blaming anyone for my mistakes. I take full responsibility for anything I do in life. But I did learn that doing business overseas is very dangerous, and there are lots of sharks out there who will eat you up and spit you out.

So it was with my tail between my legs that I went back to live with mum and dad. It was so embarrassing living at home with them when the debt collectors came knocking. To this day I feel sorry for my parents.

While I was overseas I did have one piece of good luck. Citibank rang me to say they would pay me $400 if I referred a person who subsequently obtained a loan from them. This gave me an idea. I did my research and saw that banks would soon start selling loans via third party salespeople like mortgage brokers.

I had no money and still owed my creditors over $100,000. Hardly the right start for any business, but I had a great idea and wanted to get it done. I was lucky enough to find a local investor who provided $50,000 in capital to build the software that would revolutionise the mortgage brokerage industry.

Over the next five years I went from nothing to generating over $1 million in profit and a business worth over $5 million.

My debts were paid off in full and my business was on fire. Then came the insight part. Someone I don't even know to this day sent me a video in the mail. Based upon the video, I started investigating what was happening in the financial world, and by 2005 I knew I had to sell my business. I did, and then three years later the 2008 Global Financial Crisis hit. My business was already sold. Good luck or good planning? I will leave that to you to decide.

The lesson here is that I have immersed myself in information and refuse to take advice from the mainstream media or the so-called experts.

If I could see the GFC coming, why did experts not see it also?

That is why I am writing this book. The property market is just part of a giant worldwide Ponzi scam that will eat up and spit out anyone who does not wake up and start getting a real education.

And it was with this concept that my wife and I started Money Wars TV in 2010 to help people just like you get a real financial education, so that you can survive the coming financial Armageddon.

If you have picked up this book, then you have already distinguished yourself from the other 95% of people who just don't know where to start. So congratulations—you have come a long way already.

The top 5% of people in the world have actually devoted time and energy to designing their lives, and books like this are a crucial way of starting your journey.

Everyone has personal ideas about success and what it means. Some people dream of being millionaires or having enough money to retire in the style they wish. Others simply want to provide for their families while still having time to really enjoy life and devote time to loved ones or causes they care about.

Financial success is sometimes looked down upon by people who say it is based only on greed and ego.

I argue the opposite: that in fact you must survive, and the best way to survive (and thrive) is to succeed financially first, and then apply that success to other parts of your life that mean the most to you.

Personally, I just wanted to generate enough passive income (I will go into this later in the book) to allow me the freedom to spend time on what I felt was important in life, be it spending time with my partner and my kids, or just travelling somewhere whenever I desired to.

I know a lot of people—some rich, some poor—and they *all* have issues that arise with their partners, family, friends or work environments.

Everyone has issues in life. There is only thing that distinguishes the rich from the poor. Rich people can spend money on solving their problems. And they can also afford an "escape" at times to go enjoy life despite the problems (not that I advocate avoiding your problems, but a break can be healthy and provide perspective!)

Whether you like it or not, it is better to be unhappy with money than unhappy and poor.

At any rate, well done on reading this book, and I hope you enjoy your journey. It would be my honor to inspire you to take the next step on the road to success and happiness, for you and your family.

Take a moment and check out www.moneywars.tv and the must-see documentary *Money Wars*.

Enough about me. Please sit down, get comfortable and enjoy reading this challenging and provocative book.

I get a real high out of helping people who want to be helped, so if you are one of those people, or if you have any questions or comments, please feel free to email me at richard@fintrack.com.au.

CHAPTER 1

HISTORY OF MONEY

Money: is anything that is generally accepted as payment for goods and services and repayment of debts. The main uses of money are as a medium of exchange, a unit of account, and a store of value. Some authors explicitly require money to be a standard of deferred payment. The dominant form of money is currency.

– Wikipedia

"None are more hopelessly enslaved than those who falsely believe that they are FREE!"

- Johann Wolfgang von Goethe
1749 - 1832

All modern money is debt, created when a central or private bank makes a loan. So the amount of money in society is equal to the amount of debt (*total* debt, not just government debt).

Most people don't know much about the history of money or the way it is created. So what is money? Money is supposedly anything that is accepted as a medium of exchange. Before money was accepted people had a barter system where you exchange a cow for wheat etc, both parties wanted something from the other person. This created the concept of intrinsic value, which is the key to understanding the various forms of money that evolved from the barter process.

COMMODITY MONEY

Commodity Money is items such as food that have intrinsic value and hence were used as a medium of exchange. Man then learned how to refine precious metals such as iron, copper, tin, and bronze. Merchants freely traded these new metals. Values were originally made via how much the metal weighed and then later on by the number. These metals were good because they were not perishable and not too hard to carry. Gold and Silver over the years have been the most prevalent of the metals accepted as money.

RECEIPTED MONEY

Not long after the Goldsmiths experimented with paper money. For most people it was too hard to carry around gold coins so the Goldsmiths encouraged people to leave their gold with them in exchange for a written receipt, which entitle the owner to withdraw the gold at any time. Later the Goldsmiths add the word "PAY THE BEARER ON DEMAND" so that the owner of the gold could actually sell it to another person who then presented the receipt to the Goldsmith and picked up the Gold.

FIAT MONEY

This is paper money decreed by law as legal tender, not backed any gold or silver. Basically the Government makes a law that this paper must be accepted as legal tender for goods and services.

FRACTIONAL MONEY

The Goldsmiths soon realised that most depositors actually came in to collect their gold. This gave them the idea to lend out the gold they held on behalf of the depositors for more profit. In the early days most Goldsmiths were Christians and could not lend money and charge interest, this was called USUARY and was not allowed by the Church. The Jews had a similar idea but also had a loophole being that while a Jew could not charge interest on a loan to another Jew they could however charge interest on a loan to say a Christian. This is how the first Goldsmiths started lending out the gold to potential borrowers.

Then the depositors found out what the Goldsmiths were doing so they demanded part of the action in order for the Goldsmiths to legally do what they were doing. Hence the Goldsmiths began to act as loan brokers on behalf of their depositors. Over time this unsocial practice was legistimised by the Governments of the day and the Goldsmiths evolved into Banks.

FRACTIONAL MONEY RESERVE BANKING

Most borrowers want paper money rather than bulky coins so when they received the coins they simply deposited back with the Goldsmiths and you guessed it the Goldsmiths issued them with receipted paper money and then lent the coins out again to the next borrower and so on. Over time the so-called receipted paper money that was originally backed 100% by gold ended up well and truly backed by a fraction of this. This was the beginning of *fractional money* and the process by which they were created is called the *fractional reserve banking.*

The Goldsmiths who now had reinvented themselves into Banks then became very smart on how to make more money and developed the Bond market. This allowed Governments to issue Bonds or I.O.U's to raise cash to cover the shortfall of tax revenue and government spending. Bonds became the ultimate tool to raise money for war, in fact if a country cannot raise money from Bonds then they cannot wage war.

Let's take a pause and look at this Fractional Reserve lending really closely, pay attention, as this is the most important part. **Basically the Goldsmiths became Wizards and created money out of thin air.** This is the fundamental ingredient for the **current Monetary System** that the world's financial markets operate under today.

So how is it that money can be created out of thin air and how does that affect you? Well Each and every time a bank makes a loan new bank credit is created. The process by which banks create money is so simple that it is disturbing to the average person who works so hard for their money.

No one ever teach us about what money is or how the monetary system works. Perhaps we should be educating ourselves more if we want to survive in the future.

So where does money come from? Most people believe that money is created by the Government printing presses. Well this is partially true. The Government mint produces the notes and coins we use.

Private corporations known as Banks via their loans create the vast majority of money. You probably think that the Bank lends out money deposited by other people that it actually has in its vaults. But this is not correct remember the Goldsmiths? Well the bank actually lends money based upon the borrowers promise to pay it back, like an I.O.U.

The borrower signs the Mortgage documents whereby they promise to pay back the original principal loan and also the interest and fees applicable as per the agreement or they lose the security that was put up for the loan be it a house or car etc.

So basically the Bank creates money out of thin air. This is too farfetched for you to comprehend? Well it is true. The Bankers and the Government agree to what is known as "the Fractional Reserve System" where by the Bankers agreed to be regulated and to only create new money based upon a percentage of actual deposits held by the bank. The US makes banks maintain 10% as a statutory reserve but in some countries it is Nil! Do you know what statutory reserve deposit your banks have to have? Might be worth asking the question as the lower the reserve the more likely the problems in the future.

So over the years the basic character of money has changed from representing a store of value to now representing debt. The Government has allowed what is known as FIAT (money by decree) currency, which is paper money, legalised as acceptance of any debt.

New money is now created when someone takes out a loan. And what is worse is that the deposits you make to the bank are actually you lending money to the bank that then lends out your money tenfold based upon the agreed fractional reserve ratio of that bank.

SO IN A NUTSHELL HERE IS HOW IT WORKS

When the Government spends more money than it raises in taxes it borrows the difference by selling interest bearing I.O.U's such as US Bonds. When a US bank buys a US $100 Bond it gets to loan out nearly 10 times the amount as agreed by the Government of the day and the banks, so not only does the Bank get back the $100 investment plus interest from the Federal Government it gets to loan out ten times that amount that it does not have and charge additional interest.

The Banks are allowed to create this money out of thin air.

Therefore the banks are not making just say 5% on the $100 investment in US Bonds, they are actually making 5% on the $1,000 they have created as new loans which equates to over 1000% interest.

Money is created by banks, that lend to Governments, companies and people like you and me. The loans are backed by the borrowers promise to pay and hence they become portable, exchangeable and saleable assets such as Sub Prime mortgages which by now you may have heard of.

Now you know that Banks do not lend money but rather they create it out of thin air from debt or the borrowers promise to pay. Now this is really important when you think about it, **No Debt = No Money**. Hence why everyone needs money and hocks themselves to the Banks by getting into debt from the earliest years.

Money is the lifeblood of our institutions and our society. Therefore understanding the Monetary System is critical to understand why our lives are the way they are. The Media seem to make it so intimidating to challenge the status quo that most people go along with the propaganda.

Money breaks us or makes us. Finance effects every part of our lives. Not having a financial education may have a serious impact on your ability to become wealthy.

The Monetary system runs so deep it starts at school, it attacks us when we leave school and when we get our first job, then it continues to enslave us until the day we stop work and look forward to retirement only to find out that our so called retirement money has been destroyed.

School fails to teach us how to make money, how to manage money and worst of all how to invest money. School does not teach us how to make money with money or even the basics. That is the bad news, the good news is that it is not hard to actually teach yourself how to make money, how to manage money and best of all how to make even more money with money you make.

The Monetary system provides debt to people like you and me via the creation of money out of thin air by the banks under the authority of the government. Whether you like it or not if you do not start paying attention to what I am talking about then you could well end up losing everything.

CHAPTER 2

THE FEDERAL RESERVE

CREATION OF THE FEDERAL RESERVE

$\mathcal{A}$merica has had three attempts to create a US Central Bank, with the first being in 1781 when the Bank of North America was created and secondly in 1791 The First Bank of the United States was created. Both banks were privately owned and riddled with fraud. By increasing inflation both these banks fell out of flavour and were soon to cease operations.

In desperation J P Morgan argueably the most influential banker in the early 1900's caused a crisis by claiming a bank was in trouble and the consequent run on this bank in 1907 caused a panic in the financial markets. A congressional commission headed up by Senator Nelson Aldrich who had ties to the Morgan banking cartel and even ended up marrying into the Rockefellar family, came up with the recommendation that America needed a Central bank to stop a repeat of the 1907 panic. This was the foot in the door that the Central bankers needed.

The third attempt to establish a Central Bank in America came in November 1910 when the International Bankers secretly met for nine days at the vacation estate belonging to J P Morgan on Jekyll Island off the coast of Georgia in the United States. Their main purpose was to form an International banking cartel aimed at the creation of a Central Bank in America that was the same as the Bank of England which was the Central bank in Great Britain. It was at this meeting that the draft of what is now the "Federal Reserve Act" was completed. This document was written by bankers and not lawyers.

The Banking houses attending were J P Morgan, Rockefeller, Rothschild and Warburg. They had five main objectives:

1. Reduce bank competition
2. Make Easy Credit available to everyone
3. Get bailed out by Governments using taxpayer income if they made mistakes
4. Convince people that their objectives were in the people's interest

Look at the bailouts to Wall Street today and see if you think the objectives have been achieved. Wall Street banks lost nearly US $100 billion in 2008, they received US $175 billion in government bailouts. These same banks paid out US $35 billion in bonuses and kept the remaining US $40 billion as pure profit. So in essence 1 in 5 bailout dollars was pure subsidy from the Government to the banks.

Finally after two failed attempts the third US Central bank Senator Aldrich successfully promoted the cause for America's third attempt at a Central bank, namely The Federal Reserve. In 1913 President Woodrow Wilson came to power with the backing of the banking cartel on the basis that he had pre agreed to sign in the new Federal Reserve Act and so it was two days before Christmas in 1913 the Act was passed.

"Our great industrial nation is controlled by a system of credit. Our system of credit is privately concentrated. The growth of the nation therefore and all our activities are in the hands of a few men...who necessarily, by very reason of their own limitations, chill and check and destroy genuine economic freedom.

We have come to be one of the worst ruled, one of the most completely controlled and dominated governments in the civilized world. No government by free opinion, no longer a government by conviction and the vote of the majority but a government by the opinion and the duress of small groups of dominant men"

- Woodrow Wilson (Former US President)

WHO OWNS THE FEDERAL RESERVE

Despite the name the Federal Reserve is not federally owned nor does it hold any government reserves.

The Federal Reserve System virtually controls the nation's monetary system, yet it is accountable to no one. It has no budget, it is subject to no audit, and no Congressional Committee knows of, or can truly supervise its operations.

It has no legal responsibility to be transparent or accountable to the US Government or the people of the United States of America.

So who owns the Federal Reserve?

The Fed's structure is unique compared to others in the world. The Federal Reserve is not supposed to operate to make profit and be independent of government.

12 Regional Federal Reserve banks essentially own the Federal Reserve.

- Boston
- New York
- Philadelphia
- Cleveland
- Richmond
- Atlanta
- Chicago
- St Louis
- Minneapolis
- Kansas City
- Dallas
- San Francisco

In essence it is the Private shareholders that influence the Federal Reserve and not the US Government. And who are the main individuals behind the 12 Federal Reserve Regional Banks?

· Citigroup Inc.
· J P Morgan Chase
· Bank of America Corporation
· Wachovia Corporation
· Wells Fargo & Company
· Bank One Corporation
· Taunus Corporation
· Fleet Boston Financial
· U.S. Bancorp
· ABN Amro North American Holding Company
· HSBC North America Inc.
· SunTrust Banks, Inc.
· National City Corporation
· Fifth Third Bancorp
· BB&T Corporation

And who are the main individuals behind these banks?

· The Rothschild's of England and Germany
· Moses Seif of Italy
· Lazard Freres of France
· The Warburgs of Germany
· Kuhn-Loeb of Germany
· Goldman-Sachs of the United States
· Lehman Brothers of the United States (now defunct)
· Rockefellers of the United States

"It is well the people of the nation do not understand our banking and monetary system, for if they did, I believe there would be a revolution before tomorrow morning."
- Henry Ford (Former US President)

The Fed prints money that belongs to Americans and then loan it back to them and charge interest for the pleasure.

HOW THE FED MANAGES MONEY

The Federal Reserve systems allows for the creation of loans into the banking system. Most of the loans are for companies or people and backed by security like a house or car. This creation of money and the money supply allows control over an economy.

To reduce the amount of money in the economy the process is simply reversed. The Fed sells bonds to the Public and the money flows back to the purchaser's local bank.

So a sale of $1 million bonds to the public by the Fed brings back $10 million from the economy. One of the main weapons of the Fed is **the discount rate** which is the interest rate charged to commercial banks on the loans they receive from their regional Federal Reserve Bank – **referred to as the discount window.** To expand credit the Fed lowers the discount rate or to contract it raises the discount rate.

THE FEDERAL RESERVE CAUSES THE BOOMS AND BUSTS

The public was told that the Fed would stabilise the economic boom and busts, but history has proven the complete opposite. From 1914 – 1919 the money supply doubled, then in 1920 the Fed called in loans causing a massive financial panic and runs on banks to where some 5400 banks outside of the Fed reserve system collapsed thus further consolidating the Fed's monopoly on banking.

But 1920 was just a warm up. From 1921 – 1929 the Fed again increased the Money supply by over 60% and once again made extensive loans to banks and business, but what was worse was the creation of margin loans whereby a person could put 10% down and borrow the rest to buy shares which became very popular in the roaring twenties. The catch with this loan was that it could be called in at any time, called a margin call which meant the person had to sell the shares for whatever price they could get to meet the debt.

Before October 1929 the insiders exited the stock market knowing what was about to happen and so it was on October 24th 1929 the bankers who had issued the margin loans started calling them in mass sparking a massive sell off of shares and a collapse of over 16,000 banks. This could be termed the greatest robbery of all time. What is worst was that the Fed went one step more and rather than printing more money and stimulating the economy it actually contracted the economy causing the 1929 Depression to occur

So basically we are totally reliant on the Banks lending us money to survive and without this money we would all starve, a very sobering thought and scary to most of us.

There is so much evidence that the Federal Reserve policies led to the crash of 1929. The expansion of the money supply as a means of helping the economy of England pay for World War I and the resulting wave of speculation in stocks allowed by margin loans and real estate shows enough evidence that the Federal Reserve had foreknowledge of the crash.

The policies of expansion and contraction of the Federal Reserve contributed to events that were designed to trigger the 1929 Great Depression and continue pain for the future.

So while so many lost so much there is always someone who is the opposite and makes more money out of the losses.

These were the friend's of the Federal Reserve who were forewarned as to what was coming. It is worth noting here that in any future depression there will be those who will lose fortunes and those who will make fortunes, which one will you be?

"Some of the biggest men in the United States, in the field of commerce and manufacture are afraid of something. They know there is a power somewhere, so organised, so subtle, so watchful, so interlocked, so complete, so persuasive that they had better not speak above their breath when the speak above their breath in condemnation of it"

- Thomas Woodrow Wilson
(Former President
of the United States 1913 to 1921)

THE FEDERAL RESERVE AND THE MONETISATION OF DEBT (Print & Hope)

The Federal Reserve should cause every single American to be horrified because what they are currently doing is nothing but downright criminal activity that will cost Americans dearly.

On 6th March 2009 the Federal Reserve chairman Ben Bernanke declared that the Fed would not monetises any US debt yet by 16th September 2009 some US $5 billion of US debt was monetised.

This is one great Ponzi scheme that even Bernie Madoff would be proud of. The Fed is printing money to buy US treasuries as a means of faking the US Treasury's ability to raise outside capital from places like China or other previous international buyers.

The US credit card is well and truly cut off. Remember all Ponzi schemes fall under their own weight just like Bernie Madoff's had and so to this Federal Reserve Ponzi scam will fall and hard with the end casualties of war being you and me worldwide.

THE ROLE OF THE FEDERAL RESERVE AND THE US DOLLAR

The Federal Reserve creates inflation when it issues US dollars backed by government debt. Since 1913, when Congress created the Federal Reserve, America has lost 96% of its purchasing power due to inflation.

From 1913 to 2001 the national debt grew to $6 trillion in 88 years. In the next three years it climbed to $7 trillion dollars in 2004. In just one year it climbed sharply **to over $11 trillion dollars**. The acceleration of the national debt is alarming. The corresponding loss of your purchasing power may also accelerate in the near future.

THE FEDERAL RESERVE IS A GIANT PONZI SCHEME

The Federal Reserve, the quasi-autonomous body that controls the US's money supply is a "Ponzi scheme" that created "bubble after bubble" in the US economy and needs to be held accountable for its actions. Spending the future taxes of US citizens (some not even born as yet)

In August 2009, the US Government starting monetising debt, that is the US Government started buying back its own bonds within 10 days via the US Federal Reserve buying back over 47% of the 7 year bonds at the same time that Timothy Geithner (US Secretary of the Treasury) asked Congress to raise the limit that the government could raise money.

Effectively the US Federal Reserve is printing money to buy US treasury bonds that cannot be sold to international investors due to investors thinking that America is an economic risk, you know like you lending to your mates who never pay you back.

So what is wrong with this you ask? Zimbabwe did this and in 2008 they had hyperinflation. Secondly the Government can only repay the debt, and it must repay the debt, via one of two ways, be it either **RAISING TAXES** or **HOPE FOR INFLATION.**

Chapter 3

US Housing Crash

PEOPLE LOVE HOUSES

$\mathscr{B}$y far most people's wealth is wrapped up in housing be it there private home or an investment property and hence what effect this market effects a lot of people.

Debt levels are high as people try and keep up with the "Jones" and outbid each other for property purely based on who has the best bank that will lend them more that the other guy and hence force the price of the house up.

US HOUSING BOOM AND BUST

Scary headlines and scarier statistics have enveloped the American housing boom and bust that arguably may have been a catalyst for the Global Financial Crisis starting in the first place.

I will just touch on some issues here but there are warnings for all of us from this debacle.

SO WHO WAS INVOLVED IN THIS PROCESS?

US Federal Reserve

Well first there was the US Federal Reserve System who regulated the system that allowed cheap easy credit and the low level of interest rates that encouraged borrowers to borrow large sums of debt on over inflated housing that was supposed to rise in value forever.

Fanny Mae and Freddie Mac

Then there was the Federal National Mortgage Association (Fannie Mae) and the Federal Home Loan Mortgage Corporation (Freddie Mac) the two governments created but privately owned profit making enterprises that bought and sold the mortgages that local banks had sold to consumers.

These two took up the gauntlet of "home ownership" through "affordable housing for all' especially for the low income people.

Irony comes again here, how ironic that the very people the government is trying to help, the low income or poor people, many black or Hispanic etc are the very ones being burned by the government in America irrespective of which political party is in the Whitehouse.

Man sometimes I just cannot believe how stupid and naïve some people can be when it comes to man looking after man etc. Maybe people should start looking at people's actions rather than words especially when those people start saying "trust me".

The Government and US Regulations

The regulator, the US Department of Housing and Urban Development (HUD) which was supposed to oversee and regulate Fanny Mae and Freddie Mac and thereby directly influence mortgage lending practices.

On top of this was the politics of housing, whereby everyone desired a home of their own irrespective of whether they could pay back the loan or not. The term Affordable housing comes to mind, and don't governments and the poor love to have affordable housing.

It was so big in the US it became a national issues for all to have a home at an affordable price, well the greed kicked in and destroyed those hopes.

The US Government sat by and let the monster they create become even stronger and stronger thanks to the Federal Reserve and other players in this mess.

The Government was warned on many occasions that things were getting out of hand and that this property boom could not last forever and then "wham bam" it all came down with a thud and the political blame started.

A fundamental issue for the US housing market was the politics of trying to provide housing for all especially the minority groups whom also had the lowest paid jobs if they were employed at all. I won't go into the statistics I have seen but the stats I have seen show some real eye opening stuff if you were a real banker looking to protect your loans.

It is all good for the social agenda and for people to feel better by providing housing for all especially the down trodden, but the bottom line is that if you artificially stimulate housing via false demand and free easy credit to people who are not in a position to repay the loans then you have just created a recipe for disaster in the future.

Banks

Next were the Banks who just could help themselves to lend out as much easy cheap money as they could so as to improved their profits and keep the American dream going. And with the use of Lending Insurance to protect them the Banks went on a crusade of lending without any fear of loss and the prospects of making huge amounts of money.

Ah Gordon Gecko's famous words come to mind, "Greed is good".

The Mortgage Brokers

Next were the scrupulous Mortgage Brokers or sales people who sold the dream to everyone and then signed people up on debt for the never. Remember that the demand was caused by easy credit sold by eager salespeople (mortgage brokers) paid on commission who made more money by getting you into more debt.

These guys made false declarations of income if they even verified income at all and made the most of every application they could so as to be paid in gold by their masters the banks who then made massive profits on the deals, knowing full well that they might have issues down the track.

In fact I remember doing courses on low documentation loans where the instructors advised that the clients can just declare what they earned rather than prove their income.

Then the other Bank I came to know that admitted they did not verify income of a client as that was the Mortgage Brokers job, then when asked the Mortgage Broker said that income verification was the Banks problem.

Wall Street

Wall Street then took over the sales process by repackaging and splitting a basic home loan into so many parts that no one knew who owned what. The rating companies like Moody's then came to the party and rated the debts as AAA or whatever despite not really knowing how the debt was made up of.

Once upon a time people used to roll up to their bank manager and beg him for a loan after demonstrating that they had the capacity to pay the loan back, the 20% deposit to ensure the bank have collateral or security for the loan and that they had good character in their community having been gainfully employed and homed in the same place for years.

Then they were happy when the lender fixed it for 30 years as at fair but on the high side rate of interest.

Wow have things changed, what with zero down mortgages, honeymoon rates that revert to variable rates, interest only loans, low documentation or even no documentation loans (subprime ones here).

Mankind has come a long way in the last 10 – 20 years from a beggar of finance to a junkie for debt.

Adjustable rate mortgages started the problem in the US on the back of unscrupulous mortgage brokers using predatory lending practices and banks who were keen to look the other way.

It is ironic that the US Federal Reserve that keeps statistics on all this did not have a definition of the term "predatory lending practices' but then again maybe it is harder to describe what others do badly when you yourself have done far worse.

Greedy uneducated Investors

Finally there were the investors who got sucked into this scam based upon smooth salesmen in Versace suits and the promise of great wealth, come in sucker comes to mind here.

A sidenote here is I wonder where all these slick corporate salesmen are now and what are they selling to some unsuspecting smuck?

The Borrowers themselves

Last but not least is the poor borrowers themselves, I hear you say the victims of the government, banks and mortgage brokers etc.

Well hell no! These fools knew that they could not pay back the loans they just merely live in a world of denial like the rest of us.

I mean really the person who is self employed and shows no tax but yet makes $100,000 per annum on paper needs to borrow for a loan…why not just use that real cash to do it, I mean the drug dealers do so why not those poor self employed people.

Well the truth is that they were in denial and they figured one day the house would be worth heaps and then they could just refinance again and continue the denial.

Or even worse the guy with no job who figured it would be great to get into a new home even though he had no way of paying it back, and they all screamed that the Mortgage Broker lied on the application that they themselves signed!

It is almost laughable the way people have no responsibility or accountability for their actions.

CHAPTER 4

THE COMING DEPRESSION

GREATEST ECONOMIC DISASTER IN WORLD HISTORY

$\mathcal{T}$he greatest economic convulsion in over 500 years is happening now right before your eyes today.

For hundreds of years economic cycles have struck with the **BOOMS** and **BUSTS** over time. With most of them getting bigger and bigger over the years.

In the last cycle in world history the United States and Western Europe have become the most dominate economic and military powers in the World.

Today we talk about the American Empire and its invasion of Iraq and Afghanistan, just like we used to speak about the Greek or Roman Empires.

But 2008-2009 has seen the cracks appear in the Monetary System in the US and other western countries.

The West and particularly the United States have converted themselves from manufacturers to consumers funded by huge debt binges and aided by their pimp governments borrowing record high levels of new debt to keep the consumer spending programs going.

Western people are hooked more on debt than druggies are hooked on cocaine or heroin.

This has contributed to the world economies suffering what is termed "the Global Financial Crisis (GFC)" and people around the world are continuing to suffer.

This is not going to be like the last GREAT DEPRESSION of 1929, as we do not have the infinite resources available such as land or commodities that we had back in 1929.

Unfortunately we have used up most of our real resources such as oil and food. In the 1930's people grew their own food for survival.

A real example of how this is crucial is 1991 when the Soviet Union broke up and two countries being North Korea and Cuba felt the brunt of less oil supplies.

North Korea decided to use the planned economy and the government controlled and allocated resources for food manufacturing.

Cuba on the other hand decided to relax the planned economy style and encouraged every Cuban to use whatever land they could find and grow their own food. The difference in the end was a starving North Korea while Cubans survived.

The other marked contrast from 1929 to today is the extremely high level of debt by individuals, corporations and even countries like the United States of America.

All this adds up to a depression like the world has never seen before.

THE SEEDS OF DESTRUCTION HAVE BEEN PLANTED

The **US dollar is in real trouble** and with it goes the world. Federal planners have already gone nuclear with their printing of money and debt levels at historical highs never seen before. It has become so bad that China is reluctant to buy any more US debt.

Just looking at the Federal Reserve in America gives you a good start to seeing the math not adding up.

The Federal Reserve set up new liquidity and credit facilities to keep over committed financial firms afloat during the Global meltdown. So began the monetisation of mortgage and Treasury debt creating new Fed money to support the US housing market and the criminally reckless spending policies of the US government.

If you visit a website www.usdebtclock.org you will see the huge amount of debt that has stressed the United States and possibly the world over time.

As of **August 2012** the US national debt has reached over $16 trillion meaning that the average American has to fund over US $450,000 to clear the US debts or obligations even before Obama's government spends more on Health care reform (estimated at US $1 trillion over 10 years) and Cap & Trade programs. The maths simply does not add up.

Is there any way to pay for these programs without bankrupting America? America is in so much debt, how can they spend more borrowed money on cap-and-trade and healthcare programs before they stop the flow of red ink?

Think about this scenario that American's face today as if it was you that received the credit card from the bank and rather than spend the money on getting a job you actually gave up work and bought new clothes, an LCD and even maybe a car.

Then as the payments came due you thought about how you could make the repayments.....hmmm you were stumped as you had no job and could not pay the repayment.

Then it came to you a brilliant idea, why not borrow more money to pay the Credit Card payment. So off you went and got another loan to pay out the first loan and make some repayment.

How long do you think this would last until the lender actually discovered you were not working or simply said enough is enough and told you that there would no longer be any more money for you?

Then once you ran out of all the banks that loaned money you slumped in your chair and felt this huge emotionally feeling of, HOLY CRAP, what have I got myself into. Well this has now happened to the United States, but rather than make production and make profits they just keeping printing money on the hope that the Chinese will buy the debt.

Then WHAM, one day the Chinese and other world investor's wake up to the fact that the United States is bankrupt and the US dollar is worthless. Add to this the

fact that consumers contribute around 70% of GDP for America it just adds fuel to the fire. Well my friend that day is so near it is scary.

The prospect of the United States defaulting on its debt is not just likely, it is inevitable, and imminent. It seems that reason has disappeared on a daily basis and soon to collapse under the mass of their sheer size of mounting government debt binges.

THE ROLE OF THE FEDERAL RESERVE AND THE US DOLLAR

The Federal Reserve creates inflation when it issues US dollars backed by government debt. Since 1913, when Congress created the Federal Reserve, America has lost 96% of its purchasing power due to inflation.

From 1913 to 2001 the national debt grew to $6 trillion in 88 years. In the next three years it climbed to $7 trillion dollars in 2004. In just one year it climbed sharply **to over $11 trillion dollars**. The acceleration of the national debt is alarming.

The corresponding loss of your purchasing power may also accelerate in the near future.

Today America's debt is over $16 trillion dollars.

The interest payments only will be about **$400 billion per annum** paid to overseas investors rather than used for building America.

It is estimated that **by 2019 annual interest payments** could rise to a **projected $900 billion**.

Most economists agree the US dollar may collapse, they just disagree on when. China in 2009 stopped buying US Bonds and decided that the USA was no longer a good credit risk.

China is and will continue to unwind its US dollar investments in the coming years until it reaches a point where it does not care what happens to America, then wham bam, the Chinese will dump the US for good.

Already a world currency has been touted to replace the US dollar. Or perhaps China's currency will become the new world currency, stay tuned on that one.

HOW DID WE GET INTO THIS MESS?

Well once you understand how we got there you will be half way there to profiting from the carnage.

You see most people are followers and not leaders so most of the world is happy to be sucked in by their government deeper and deeper into slavery rather than taking a stand and demanding an end to the corruption and destruction that most governments impose.

There is no one main cause that created this GFC but rather a *system designed* and implemented by certain people who want to transform the world.

The biggest problem is that we have moved from an Economy that produces goods and services to a Casino economy where we speculate of things going up and down.

Just look at the stock market or property market where people bet on rising prices rather than real economic values.

But you say what about all those news programs you listen to that help you make an informed economic assessment of your buying and selling?

Those programs are today like sports commentators giving you blow by blow, minute by minute assessment of information that is supplied to them in a controlled form by special interest groups that make money out of your buying and selling.

Over the years a number of so called smart people who called themselves financial engineers, drew up so many ways of playing the Casino in all sorts of ways that were so complex that even the salespeople could not explain them and even a whole country Iceland become bankrupt over them.

Big trading companies in the USA and the world used algorithms and super fast computers to spot trends in financial markets before other investors saw the same opportunity. High finance became Science fiction with supercomputers the weapons of choice.

Unfortunately this so called competitive advantage only helps the small elite not the average Joe like you and me.

Somewhere along the way the world's appetite for greed overtook the business model of producing goods and services in exchange for betting, sorry investing, on financial markets as to whether these markets would go up or down.

It has become so bad that people actually bet or invest on companies or indices performing worst than the day before. Why would we as a world allow money that could be used for good like production of products, be used for destroying companies that might actually have made things that we could have used?

I have heard statistics that show that 95% of the world's money is invested in the financial markets and only 5% invested in production of goods and services.

Just look around in America and you will see how it has been transformed from a country that used to produce things to basically just consumers that are given money from the exact people who now produce the goods.

Apparently Global trade or Free trade was a part of this transformation and that it is really good for us. Well I don't see the benefit now that America does not produce anything and is shredding jobs every day. Who knows when the unemployment will stop!

I talk to people about why they want to borrow so much and buy everything and the thing that amazes me is their crowd mentality.

They cannot stand to be different to everyone else so when a friend of theirs starts to borrow to the hilt and invest, then god dam it they have to do the same or feel embarrassed that they have not been so brave or whatever.

There is so much peer pressure on everything we do to the point of self-destruction but hey who cares as long as we are all doing it then it is fine, right?

BUT MEDIA SAY THE RECESSION IS OVER!

Really, you really believe the recession is over.

Just because your government says it is over means nothing, I mean these are the guys who refused to admit they did not foresee the global financial crisis and did not have any real answers beside spend, spend and more spending.

This recession is far from over and many people worldwide are forecasting NOT a RECESSION, BUT RATHER A DEPRESSION!

Here is why I feel we are in for some really tough times:

1.   *US HOME LOAN – MORE PROBLEMS*

End of 2010 will see another massive amount of US home loans that will readjust from a fixed honeymoon rate to variable rates that are on the rise.

People will struggle to make their mortgage payments and this will result in more foreclosures and decrease in house values as demand lessens.

Then comes the banks that rely on the income (interest) that will fail a real toxic mess.

Banks who are holding distressed is artificially propping up housing and foreclosed property and they will only release small parcels into the market to stop any run on property prices.

2.   *UNEMPLOYMENT*

Unemployment is still on the rise (refer later why this will continue) with most economists believing that the real rate of unemployment is running dangerously high.

In the 1929 Depression unemployment reached 18% and today in USA they are nearly there.

There is a real chance that the Toxic debt will bankrupt many companies worldwide and then the unemployment will increase dramatically plus Governments will have to slash spending to pay for the huge deficits and there goes the government jobs.

3.   CENTRAL BANKS

Governments and central banks worldwide will continue the foolish bailouts of banks and companies that are too big to fail.

They will continue to buy up the toxic mortgage backed security loans for residential and commercial property, which at last count.

What makes this even worse is that China does not want to buy any more government debt so the Central banks like the Fed in USA are starting to buy their own government bonds, a recipe for disaster in the long term.

4.   POPULATION DEMOGRAPHICS

The last but not least issue for the West in particular is the ageing of our population in a future that will need to raise more tax revenue than ever before so as to pay for the massive government debt, rising healthcare as people get older and the downright stupidity of governments who think they can run companies let alone run a country.

I see a future for the West of few too many people to pay for the oldies, and by the way I am 51 years old so I may end up one of those oldies that society will choose to either look after or help go to the grave sooner.

Have a look at US President Obama's healthcare plan and see what I mean, his plan starts with the old but may end up as similar to the film "Logan's Run".

Go out and rent this film and you may get a new understanding of what may happen in the future.

DEFINING DEPRESSION

So what is a Depression?

An economic contraction begins with a deficiency of total demand for goods and services in relation to their total production, valued at current prices. When such a deficiency develops, prices for goods and services fall.

Falling prices are a signal to producers to cut back production with a resulting total decline in overall production.

The difference between a "Recession" and a "Depression" depends on the overall decline in production.

In my view the overall decline will be large enough for ALL economists to clearly agree to call the coming contraction the "GREATEST DEPRESSION EVER".

THE GREAT PONZI SCHEME – US FEDERAL RESERVE (Central Banks)

Imagine becoming so successful at your job that you stack up $2 trillion in income, which you conservatively place in short-term U.S. Treasury bonds for safekeeping. Now imagine that when you try to cash in those bonds to buy a few things for your kids, the clerk at the bank abruptly shuts her window and tells you to go away.

That is essentially the situation faced by China these days as it wonders whether its plan to manufacture goods for U.S. consumers over the past two decades in exchange for a pile of credit slips was really such a hot idea.

The answer is coming up as a big, fat "uh-oh" as the U.S. deficit and debt obligations balloon to levels never before contemplated, and Beijing is denied requests to buy U.S. and Australian mines and oil properties.

And as Beijing leaders talk openly, if obliquely, about their angst, they are unsettling world credit, currency and stock markets, which don't know what to make of the idea that the world's largest Ponzi scheme might be coming to an abrupt end.

This is a good time to assess the chilling possibilities, as the resolution of this pending crisis will afflict investors, workers and business owners alike.

So basically the government hopes for inflation as this will mean that their 10% tax is not on $1,000 BUT rather 10% on $10,000 or more, you get the point.

In other words **the Government wants INFLATION** and hence works with the so called independent central banks to stay off inflation in public while behind the scenes they plot to increase Inflation at your peril.

SOCIAL SECURITY and MEDICARE ARE THE NEXT PONZI SCHEMES

Lets look at America for an example. The US government has some $14 trillion in unfunded liability for social security.

The reason why it is the next Ponzi scheme is that we have now hit a tipping point where millions of baby boomers will begin retiring and collecting money from the government at the same time we will have less taxpayers, not good I say.

But there is more, yes in America they also have Medicare, which has some $68 trillion in unfunded liabilities.

The government in America has promised the taxes from generations to come to pay for their social security and Medicare programs.

THE DEMAND FOR RESOURCES

As China and India try to grow and the world's population expands at its current growth, demand for commodities like food, water and oil will go through the roof. There simply is not enough of stuff to feed, clothe and shelter everyone.

Hence demand side inflation will cause massive increases in the amount you pay for life's basics such as electricity, water, food and even worse Oil. Here are some reasons why commodity prices will surge:

- Population growth continues and with it food and water requirements
- China and then India needs to house its people
- Gas guzzling cars will still be around despite Governments refuting this
- Cap and Trade schemes will force higher costs

The world simply cannot keep up to meet the needs of the population, not on this planet anyway.

INFLATION IS THE GOVERNMENTS FRIEND AND WHY THEY WANT IT

Governments love inflation as it allows them to take money from you without you even knowing it.

So why would the government secretly want to take your money, which is what happens when the central bank expands the money supply by creating money and thereby causing inflation and hence reducing the value of dollars you own?

Government love creating inflation because:
- *makes paying national debt easier as it is repaid with cheaper dollars*
- *allows governments to pursue monetary policy to accommodate special interest groups*

- *inflation finances social programs that are adjusted for inflation rather than raising taxes*
- *corrupting statistics with inflation creates the myth of economic growth*
- *inflation causes shares and property to increase thus instilling the illusion of wealth*

HOW HIGH COULD INFLATION GO?

Many people have little memory of inflation but from 1970's to 1980's the World had very high inflation. In fact many people had illusionary wealth during this time.

Since the 1990's the government has apparently managed the inflation rate but I disagree.

I believe they have merely manipulated the rate of inflation by playing with the criteria and that is why you shake your head when inflation is 1.5% and food prices go up by 10% in a week.

WHAT ABOUT HYPERINFLATION

The US Federal Reserve policy of spending its way out of this Global Financial Crisis will have a long-term impact on the US and other economies of the world.

Will we see hyperinflation like in Argentina and Germany pre World War II?

STRESS TEST - CAN YOU COPE WITH RISING INTEREST RATES

Inflation is the driver of higher interest rates. So the recession is over according to the Government and media.

I suggest you do your own mortgage stress test just like they did on US banks in 2009. Do the math and calculate your current mortgage at 10%, 15% and 20% and see how long you would last.... I hear you screaming that there is no way can interest rates get to 20% let alone 10%.

Well don't YOU have a poor memory, just look back at history and see how high interest rates can go.

Have I got you thinking right now that maybe you would be struggling to repay the home loan?

Well you are not alone and what's worse is that the price of the home your live in could drop some 20% to 40% just like in Europe and USA.

WAKE UP NOW BEFORE IT IS TOO LATE

Why not tax the rich and give to the poor, taxes are the politician weapon of choice. Governments will have to start taxing the rich as they run out of ways to create money to pay for all their services and what is worse is that you will be paying more for all your services and getting fewer services.

SOMEONE HAS TO PAY FOR ALL THIS SPENDING RIGHT?

Basically someone has to pay for less government revenue, more government spending and record public and private debt and my friend that could be you.

Already in Australia the government is looking at a "wealth tax" on people who own homes over $2 million. I hear you say that that is right, well just wait for a moment as if you start letting the government do this then they can do anything they want.

Did you know that income tax in America was only meant to be for the wealthiest 1% in 1913 but quickly grew to 5% in 1939 and then following World War II, to almost 65% federal and state tax?

Also the worst part of taxing the rich is that once the rich are poor like the rest of the people then who will pay then? Yep we need the rich to make money so the poor can be looked after.

DEFLATION AND DEPRESSION GO TOGETHER

Depressions are characterised in part by a persistent sustained general decline in production.

This decline reduces the ability for people to earn money, repay debts, or invest in business. Because both credit (no one wants to lend at any interest rate) and production (of goods and services) support prices for investment assets, the prices of assets will fall in a deflationary depression.

As asset values fall people lose wealth, which reduces their ability to offer credit, service debt
or support production. This mix of forces is self reinforcing and very destructive.

Unless drastic measures are taken almost immediately the world economy will collapse. Let me just enlighten you to three main drivers I see that paint a very interesting picture.

The Amount of Money pumped into the economy by Government stimulus spending

The amount of money pumped into the system has increased dramatically.

The Amount of money speculated on shares and property (i.e. the Casino)

Speculators have spent all their money on shares and property betting they will go up forever.

The Amount of Actual production – real economy that feeds us

Since 2000 the government has pumped in more money into the system to keep it afloat at a faster rate, the beginning of hyperinflation. Under hyperinflation what essential is happening is that the money is losing its value at an increasing rate so therefore you have to pump more money in to get the same effect.

This is when the monetary system starts to break down.

In 2007 to 2009 the financial system started to fall apart and the start of deflation of assets so the government pumps in money (bailout) and hence we have deflation and hyperinflation at the same time which causes the collapse of the physical production as seen in lost jobs, company collapses, bankruptcies.

The bottom line is that the physical production in America is collapsing and hence is the doom of the United States unless it is reversed. This is the death of the monetary system and no bailout will save us.

CHAPTER 5

FINANCIAL EDUCATION

INVEST IN YOURSELF

In my opinion investing in yourself is the only real investment that you cannot lose on. I have spent thousands on my education and I am not talking about school.

The money I have spent on myself has been repaid many folds.

Even today I still spend money on my very own personal education including subscribing to numerous newsletters, magazines and other information services.

The money you spend on this program will save you thousands of dollars in interest and debt if you apply my strategies as directed. Financial education is the best value for money you will ever get.

GET A FINANCIAL EDUCATION

We've all heard these stories like this before, but here is an example of what might happen and there's a very important lesson here for you.

A guy named "Bud" in the U.S won $16.2 Million in the lottery and within twelve months he was completely broke and $1 million dollars in debt!

Now he wishes it never happened! Here's what happened...

1. A former girlfriend sued him for a share of it (not his only lawsuit)
2. A brother was arrested for hiring a hit man to kill him for the money
3. Other siblings harassed him to invest in their business, which failed!

Bud eventually pleaded bankruptcy 12 months later and now lives on $450 a MONTH plus food stamps.

He admits to being both careless and foolish (Nah really?). Statistics show that 90% of lottery winners who win over $500,000 are back to square one (or worse) within 12 months plus have a trail of broken relationships along the way. As you read further, you'll find out why. But first let is look at the flip side. Smart Guy, 34, a manager for a local Gym looks at his expenses and identifies the GOOD expense from the BAD expenses and creates a surplus of money to apply to his debts

One debt at a time he applies his financial and emotional energy until one day after all his hard work **he is DEBT FREE.**

His surplus is still there and in fact he has increased his income via a home business and his overall cash surplus is larger than ever.

He sits in his chair watching his children play and feels the huge relief of his house and cars been owned outright and his ability to spend a little money on his kids when he wants.

Then comes the story of Bud and his heart sinks and he feels for poor Bud.

Because Smart Guy knows that the only difference between Bud and himself is one thing, Simple financial education. The best news is that this is a skill that can be learned easily.

Bud still lives in FEAR of what life will bring, while SMART GUY enjoys his wife and kids everyday. Who would you like to be?

INCOME AND EXPENDITURE STATEMENT

The Income & Expense statement can be scary for some when they complete this statement as it shows you how little you earn and how much you spend.

This is a fundamental basic tool that identifies what you earn and what you spend.

The poor focus on a JOB and earn income for their Income & Expenditure Statement. The Rich focus on buying Assets to generate income for their Income & Expenditure Statement.

We all have choices to buy an Asset or an Expense. The key is to have money work for you and not have you work for money.

Oh and above all don't get sucked in to the old sayings like

JOB = SECURITY or GOVERNMENT = LOOKING AFTER ME

As I am the cynical person I don't think your boss or the Government really care about you or your family.

All income is generally good but not all expenses are bad, some are Necessities and some are Luxuries.

You need to identify expenses that can be removed from the day-to-day bills and free up surplus cash flow so as to apply this to your debts as per my formula for becoming debt free.

Remember your next holiday may be in your daily coffee or your financial independence may be in your closet.

Don't let EGO get in the way of financial freedom. Try and control your spending and certainly don't use debt such as credit cards or personal loans to get what you want.

Most spending is emotional and comes at a cost of what you could have done with that money had you used it more wisely.

"Most people with big Egos' have small bank balances."

ASSET AND LIABILITY STATEMENT

The Author of the world famous "Rich Dad, Poor Dad" Robert Kyiosaki sums it up so well when he said, *"Assets feed me, Liabilities eat me "*.

It is so true, every time you buy an asset that makes you money your bank balance goes up, and every time you get something on credit your interest and repayments eat you alive.

There is a difference between Income producing assets and non-income producing assets. For example your home is an example of a NON-INCOME producing asset and in fact it costs you to hold this asset, whereas the Investment property would be INCOME producing and hence a better asset to purchase.

Now some of you are thinking, hang on Richard our adviser said we need debt to invest and sometimes they are right. You see there is **Good Debt** and **Bad Debt.**

But remember only two generations ago people bought assets with cash and no debt.

SPENDING IS EMOTIONAL

An example of bad debt is when Dumb Person goes to the shops and buys some stuff (you know new LCD TV or brand new watch etc) and then Dumb Person places it on the credit card.

Wow Dumb Person feels great and watches TV with pleasure and even wears the watch and shows people how good it looks.

Then comes the next month's credit card statement and hopefully Dumb Person can pay it off, if not then Dumb Person starts getting a high interest rate being applied to his credit card and the struggle to pay Dumb Person debts starts to mount.

Often it gets so bad that Dumb Person needs to sell something to pay off the credit card or even worse has to borrow more, yep you guessed it, Dumb Person has to sell the TV or the Watch for 50% of the original value if Dumb Person is lucky.

So here we have an example of Dumb Person going off and buying something for pleasure (and I know it is fun, I have been there and done it) but only to end up in crying and shame unlike the Smart Person.

Good Debt = Debt used to buy an asset that feeds your Short-term gratification OR Long term rewards

LOWER YOU'RE COST OF LIVING

Take a hard look at your budget and look at your cost of living. Identify all your expenses as Luxury, Discretionary or necessity, and then cut out as many expenses as you can.

Look at websites that help you save money so that the end result is that you free up spare net income every month to apply towards your debts.

PAY OFF YOUR DEBTS SOONER

Make extra payments
However you receive extra funds. Whether it is through inheritance, a lottery win, a bonus from work, a tax return, the sale of other assets, this money is best spent on your mortgage.

Redirecting funds straight into your mortgage instead of into your day-to-day account will assist with the overall reduction in your long-term financial commitment.

Pay more regularly

Numerous financial institutions have facilities that allow you to set up an automatic crediting system. This allows you to redirect funds from one account into your mortgage.

Increase your payments

All financial institutions stipulate a minimum monthly payment made to serve a loan. If you pay above this rate, then you are reducing the life of your loan.

If you increase the payment made on your mortgage then you are effectively reducing the interest charged each month on the principal amount.

In order to make this sort of commitment each month you must take into account your overall monthly expenditure and factor this additional payment into your budget.

Find a lower interest rate

The rate of interest charged on your mortgage can be the difference between paying it off quickly as opposed to numerous years.

Interest rates fluctuate in line with economic boom and bust periods. When deciding on a lender, choose one who offers the most flexible package and one whose interest rates are lowest.

Generally speaking extra features mean a higher interest rate. Features such as a redraw facility can add to the interest rate you are charged.

Think carefully about the features you need because if you have a loan with features you do not use, then you can pay a higher interest rate and therefore more interest over the life of the loan.

Consolidate your debts when appropriate

In a financial climate where interest rates fluctuate and the degree of fluctuation can greatly influence the ability to service a loan, whether it is a home, car or personal loan.

Coupled with higher rates of interest attached to loans are the ones attached to credit cards.

If you have numerous loans with a variety of lenders, chances are you are paying off more in interest than if you were to consolidate your loans into one and have the loan charged at one rate than three or four.

Become debt free

Become Debt Free over time by using your spare net income that is created out of lowering your cost of living.

ou would be amazed at how much you could save from a few hundred dollars applied to your debts every month.

Remember no one can sell up your home if you don't owe anyone any money.

Here is a basic formula for paying off debts that I feel works really well.

A BUDGET IS YOUR KEY TO SUCCESS

Create a Budget

You need to find out how much spare cash you have to apply to your mortgage. In order to do this you need to create a budget including all your income and expenses and then identifying your true net cash surplus or loss.

If you don't have any surplus income then let Fintrack find some through our budget assessment process.

Then once we have free up some cash we can then apply this to the loan and so save you thousands of dollars over the term of the loan.

Find the surplus in your budget
You need to find the **surplus money** that you have tied up in your cash flow so as to use this to reduce your debts.

You must be honest with yourself and look at the money you waste on luxuries compared to necessities of life.

We all do it so don't feel ashamed, society has conditioned you to the world of consumerism and lifestyle.

So remember we looked at expenses and determined which are a NECESSITY and which are LUXURY.

Now remember any expense is subject to your interpretation of what you believe is a Necessity and a Luxury, the only difference between your definition and mine is whether you want to become debt free and escape slavery.

Just because you have the money in your bank account does not mean you have to spend it or get more debt to spend more.

Use the budget surplus to reduce your debts
Ok now you know how much surplus you have per week or month to starting reducing your debts and finally end financial slavery to debt.

What are you going to spend this surplus on?

This is where we discuss GOOD spending and BAD spending.

Good Spending (if there is any)
Good spending WILL give you a return on your money today or in the future. Investing in an asset that makes money or investing in training for your future are examples of good spending.

Bad Spending (there is plenty of this going around)

Bad spending WILL NOT make a return on your money today or in the future.

Buying a second pair of shoes or buying golf clubs may make you feel better or improve your golf handicap but it will not make you any money and will keep you a slave to debt.

Once you have mastered your debt and eradicated your debt slavery you can then if you have to buy the shoes or golf clubs with your surplus money without emotional guilt and know you have paid cash for the goods.

GENERATE MORE INCOME

Try and start a low cost business to generate more income. Then use this new income in your budget.

If successful you can use the extra income to pay off as much debt as possible. Most people are scared to start a new business especially if they are working full time.

Well unless you win a lottery or your boss gives you a pay rise you may find it really hard to pay your bills. Good luck and if run into troubles email me richard@fintrack.com.au.

CHAPTER 6

INVEST IN YOURSELF!

START YOUR FINANCIAL EDUCATION NOW

$\mathscr{O}$k so lets start getting you the financial education that you need and you can do what ever you like with it, but be warned after finishing your financial education you will have a choice that will impact on you for the rest of your life and most probably the rest of your childrens lives.

Good luck and listen carefully.

Inflation is the driver of higher interest rates. So the recession is over according to the Government and media, ok so why not do your own mortgage stress test just like they did on US banks in 2009.

Do the maths on your own debts and see if you can survive interest rates over 10%.

You probably don't believe that interest rates will go that high but history would indicate that they can and with it comes a lot of foreclosures and pain for homeowners with debt.

Have I got you thinking right now that maybe you would be struggling to repay the home loan?

Well you are not alone and what's worse is that the price of the home your live in could drop some 20% to 40% just like in Europe and USA.

INVESTING IN THE SHARE MARKET

Don't believe what the financial experts tell you about how good the stock market is or that day trading or renting shares are good investments.

You have no control over the investment and there are the CEO's on huge pay packets and bonuses linked to their goals and not yours, plus there is the lack of transparency of any real reporting.

We have had some 7 major crashes in the past 100 years with each one getting worse than the previous crash.

And in most of these crashes there was a major corporation that was corrupt to the core and aided by the Government lack of regulation.

Remember ENRON, once a small US gas company based in Houston Texas, that went on to become the 5th biggest corporation in the world and the darling of Wall Street.

Enron promised to revolutionise the energy business. Riding a wave of Energy deregulation Enron started buying up companies all over the world.

Enron lead a Wall Street surge and assisted by the old friend the Federal Reserve Bank who kept interest rates low to allow cheap easy finance for Enron and their shareholders alike.

Enron turned out to be a complete fraud what with energy manipulations of the quantity and price of energy combined with the most corrupt business accounting ever seen in America.

So basically corporations cooking their books and rigged stock markets assisted by corrupt government officials have led to successive massive scams in our stock markets and what is worse is that people love to get involved in the greed and use debt to fund their investments.

So why do we have so many booms and busts with the share market. One answer is the herd mentality where we as humans act upon fear and loose all rational thinking.

In a nutshell I think it is not much better than the casino, hence why I refer to it as a Casino. In fact I heard that in the United States some of their share brokers get information before the public does and hence they trade the market before the YOU and I can and that is not good for you.

The events of 2008/2009 show how risky this investment can be. If you must buy shares do it with cash and only invest in shares that have regular proven dividends.

Don't borrow to gear up your investment.

INVESTING IN PROPERTY

Property has supposedly been the greatest investment and considered by most as safe as bricks and mortar. In most times you could buy a property and sell it years later for a possible profit. If you really know how to invest in the property market then you can still do well, but for most of us we are deluding ourselves that we can make money when the market is volatile.

People over time have found that buying property has been predominately bought to protect against risk. Insurance failed, the welfare state failed and the derivative markets seemed too risky so property became the best option to protect investors against risk and hence create wealth.

And the worst part of property investment is the huge debt created. Oh and by the way if you think you own the property then think again as if you have a debt then the bank owns the property.

For all the talk about property being excellent value and a great long term investment, I believe that property buyers actually don't have any interest in the property they're buying.

In fact, I'd go so far as to say that property buyers are not buying property at all. Rather, they are 'buying' a loan and using the house as security.

It seems that the actual house is a secondary consideration. The problem with property is that investors see a house as an investment rather than a house to live in.

So property investors go out and borrow more money than the next property investor or potential home buyer and then use this debt to outbid everyone so as to end up with an inflated property value.

It really is so similar to investing in the Casino, I mean stock market, where everyone is betting on the asset value increasing forever and ever irrespective of real reasons rather than speculative investment.

The speculator adds money to the stock market via buying and selling of shares rather than relying on company cash flows or balance sheets, they buy because they believe the price will rise - nothing more, nothing less.

Property investing is the same. Many people buy a house because they want to live in it, and because they prefer ownership to renting.

However, more and more, property buyers and home owners have been brainwashed by the 'location, location, location' mantra.

They are buying not because they want a place to live, but because they believe the price/value will rise.

They buy not because it is close to the train station for their own benefit but because they are told it will 'add value' when they sell.

They don't buy because it is close to the shops, but because it will 'add value' when they sell. Even though the buyers are just as likely to drive a car to the station or the shops.

In most cases people buy the property based upon someone telling them there is so much demand building up that the property has to rise in value, rather than discussing the merits of what the property is all about or how much a renter would love to rent the place and therefore pay rent.

The biggest issue is that people take on huge debt levels well above what their incomes can service on the pretence that the house price always goes up just like in Europe and America, well this is very dangerous.

It is no different to other countries in the world and will see reduction in home values as people realise this big scam that is being peddled by everyone from the mortgage broker, real estate agent, bank right through to the vender and potential buyers themselves who are unwitting participants in this scam.

One of the comments that people refer to is: *"There must be a shortage of houses because house prices have gone up. If there was a surplus of housing then prices would fall. Simple as that."*

Well I wish it was that simple but it is not, property prices only go up if there is money available to the buyers and as I explain in this book, as the monetary system crashes so will the cheap money for property investors.

This is going to shock the absolute foundation belief of property as people see not only property prices not rise but actually reduce in value.

LESSONS FROM EUROPE AND USA

The examples of Europe and USA scare me. The lessons of 2008 and 2009 show how easy it is for a person's home to become a debt trap.

The risk of rising unemployment and higher interest rates soon cause negative equity into a property.

Negative equity is where your debt is larger than the value of your home.

It was said that in places like Detroit people just abandon their houses. Foreclosure filings in the United States are stilling rising ever higher and overwhelming any futile efforts by the US government.

Nearly some 1 million homes per year are being foreclosed on, it is estimated that some 3 million homes.

Naturally the fall in house prices led to massive rise in mortgage defaults and foreclosures and hence increase the supply of houses onto the American market when prices were falling.

The result was massive losses by homeowners and banks.

The banks suffered badly due to the American system whereby if you hand back the keys to the bank before you are in trouble the Bank can only sell the house and not go after you for any negative equity.

Hence why so many Americans just quit their houses and ran for the high ground.

CAN YOU TRUST YOUR FINANCIAL ADVISORS OR YOUR INSTINCT

How many of you have been sold the big dream about property by the real estate salesman, or told how shares are best by your stockbroker or worst still you sought advice from a Financial Planner who received commissions from the investment companies they put you in.

Well I think most of us have been there and done that, and now with the global credit crisis the same people are saying that they are not to blame, but that it is a world problem.

Well maybe there is some truth in this but the bottom line for most of these salespeople is that they have or are still receiving commissions for selling you the investments and now the investments have gone bad they accept no responsibility for their actions.

I have watched people work so hard for their retirement only to find out that the financial expert put them into a product that made them money but lost money for the retiree, and then to top it off the government allowed it as it was apparently legal.

Well I guess it is easier to steal with a pen than a gun nowadays.

Just have a look at the property groups, banks and other financial experts in American, Europe and Australia today and see how many of them have made their money while others have lost their life savings...I would not even dare to put a list up as it would take too long to make the list. Let alone the US bailouts to companies that were too big to fail, I mean give me a break.

How many of you have been sold the big dream about property by the real estate salesman, or told how shares are best by your stockbroker or worst still you sought advice from a Financial Planner who received commissions from the investment companies they put you in.

Well I think most of us have been there and done that, and now with the global credit crisis the same people are saying that they are not to blame, but that it is a world problem.

Well maybe there is some truth in this but the bottom line for most of these salespeople is that they have or are still receiving commissions for selling you the investments and now the investments have gone bad they accept no responsibility for their actions.

Well maybe you need to think twice before accepting someone's advice in the future especially if they are being paid commission relative to the investment being made. I will add that NOT ALL professional people are like this.

INVEST IN YOURSELF

In my opinion investing in yourself is the only real investment that you cannot lose on. I have spent thousands on my education and I am not talking about school. The money I have spent on myself has been repaid many folds.

Even today I still spend money on my very own personal education including subscribing to numerous newsletters, magazines and other information services.

The money you spend on this program will save you thousands of dollars in interest and debt if you apply my strategies as directed.

Financial education is the best value for money you will ever get. I thank you for reading this book and if you have any questions please email me at richard@fintrack.com.au and take time to check out www.moneywarstv. com.

www.ingramcontent.com/pod-product-compliance
Lightning Source LLC
LaVergne TN
LVHW021547080426
835509LV00019B/2885